Strength & Valor
A Kid's Guide To Valencia, Spain

Photography by John D. Weigand
Poetry by Penelope Dyan

Bellissima Publishing, LLC
Jamul, California
www.bellissimapublishing.com

Copyright © 2016 by Penny D. Weigand and John D. Weigand

All rights reserved. No part of this book may be
reproduced or transmitted in any form or by any means,
electronic or mechanical, including photocopying,
recording, or by any other means, or by any information or
storage retrieval system, without permission from the publisher.

ISBN 978-1-61477-264-4
First Edition

The aim of art is to represent not the outward
appearance of things,
but their inward significance.

ARISTOTLE

Strength & Valor
Bellissima Publishing, LLC

Introduction

Valencia is the third largest city in Spain, after Madrid and Barcelona. Founded as a Roman colony in 138 BC, it got its name from the Romans. (The city's name 'Valencia' means strength and Valor, honoring Roman soldiers.) The middle ages saw the invasion of the Germanic peoples and overtaking by the church which changed Roman buildings into religious buildings. The city then surrendered without a fight to invading Moors in 714 AD. In 1238, King James I of Aragon, with armies of Aragonese, Catalans, Navarrese and crusaders from the Calatrava order, laid siege to Valencia. On September 28, the city surrendered. A mixture of Jewish, Christians and Muslims were all allowed to remain in the city as history moved forward. What we have today is a beautiful city filled with art, culture, diversity and a lot of fun things for a kid to see and to do!

You can see some of what award winning author, attorney and former teacher, Penelope Dyan and photographer, John D. Weigand saw on their visit to Valencia, Spain, as you turn the pages of this 'learn to read' book filled with word repetition, word recognition and rhyme. Then, to see even more of this city, you can watch the free music video that goes with this book that you can find on the Belissimavideo YouTube channel.

Strength & Valor
Bellissima Publishing, LLC

Strength & Valor
A Kid's Guide To Valencia, Spain

Photography by John D. Weigand
Poetry by Penelope Dyan

This isn't a spaceship,
and it DIDN'T just land.
It's a building
in the City of Arts and Sciences,
beautiful AND grand!
Reina (Queen) Sofía Palace of the Arts,
stands as a centerpiece
of this amazing place,
that looks like something plucked
from outer space!

And all the lines and the trees,
and the continuous art on display,
will make you feel speechless,
as you move forward on your way.

And as you leave,
you find a balcony with a view,
with simple pots filled with green,
that seem set out just for you.

The streets all seem to talk,
as you set out upon your walk.

El Mercado Central,
Valencia's historic central market,
is much more than JUST a store!
It's a place filled from brim to brim,
with carne and frutas,
and surprises galore!

There are colorful scarfs for Mom!
For Dad, Mom buys a hat.
For YOU Mom buys a tee shirt.
AND you are VERY happy with that!

There are cucumbers, tomatoes,
lettuce, broccoli, radishes,
lemons sour, oranges sweet---
things that if YOU lived here,
you could buy, take home AND eat!

And there is a giant banana
drinking from a straw.
You think it's REALLY funny,
although IT'S not real at all!

Later, you see a kid just like you,
climbing with a scooter,
going up a stair or two!

And then you see
(and it's NOT small)
right in front of a STORE
stands a back and white cow!

And on a cut-off boat,
right THERE on the street.
stands a statue of a man,
with a fish AND bare feet.
Mom explains,
"It's a man pretending to be a statue,
in order to be a PART,
of the city's GREAT culture
and of the city's GREAT art!"

There are swaying palm trees,
and there are buildings high,
that stand majestically,
against the blue of the sky.

And as you leave you know
that the adventure
has JUST begun,
and tomorrow is SURE to bring
another day filled with FUN!

"Art, like beauty, lies in the eyes of the beholder. To see art, you only have to look around yourself; because art is all around you, everywhere you look... especially in the faces of those whom you love."

PENELOPE DYAN